RackGaki
落書き

RackGaki
Japanese Graffiti

Ryo Sanada // Suridh Hassan

Laurence King Publishing

LAURENCE KING

First published in 2007 by Laurence King Publishing Ltd
361-373 City Road
London EC1V 1JJ
United Kingdom

enquiries@laurenceking.co.uk
www.laurenceking.co.uk

A catalogue record for this book is available from the British Library

ISBN-13: 978-1-85669-504-6
ISBN-10: 1-85669-504-2

Research and Edit by Suridh Hassan and Ryo Sanada
Design and typeset by Ryo Sanada
All translations by Ryo Sanada
Printed in China

Cover > ESOW
Page 3 > DOPESAC + DISCAH + SASU + KAMI
Page 5 > KAMI

CONTENTS

FOREWORD

The screening of the film *Wild Style* introduced the culture of Hip Hop to Japan, but it was not until the early '90s that graffiti in Japan really took off. The main reason was Japanese going to the US, seeing graffiti and beginning to make it themselves back home.

When I started writing I was in high school. I was reading a street culture magazine under my desk during class and in the magazine there was a feature on US west coast graffiti. The work by CBS crew left a big impression on me. That was my first encounter with graffiti. The characters by EXPRESS and MEAR were overwhelming and I remember getting interested in the European graffiti scene and buying some magazines.

DELTA, ZEDZ and GASP opened my eyes to the fun of lettering and suddenly I realised I was spending all my time practising letters. But the main reason I kept writing was probably the influence of other writers who were also in my area such as PHIL, FATE and KANE. The thought that people I didn't know were writing in my area really excited me.

Japan being an island nation, information from abroad was limited. Be it good or bad, I think that fact did shape the Japanese scene into a scene of its own. Internet and magazine distribution has now spread and information is readily available. On the other hand, there are times when I think it also has become a bit boring. I sometimes think that the appeal of graffiti lies in its mystery. Styles are starting to evolve and split everywhere across this thin island nation. Many writers are now breaking the boundary and being active in their own way for self-expression rather than in the name of graffiti.

A lot of writers have left their footprints in Japan. DELTA came in the early '90s, SEEN from New York and BATES from Germany. A lot of writers came to paint in the early '90s. I still remember going to paint trains with CARS and CVES as if it was yesterday. In 1997, KOBOLT toured Japan and created a lot of commotion. His impact on Japan was massive. Other well-known writers such as TOTEM and BNHO have also visited Japan, but there are too many to mention.

In 1999, TWIST did a show in Japan. I don't think there has been a better show before or after. Since then there have been countless writers who have come to Japan to bomb or to make money.

A bit of bombing by a foreign writer now doesn't even get remembered.

Many different kinds of writers with their own ideas and ways of self-expression are about to take off and some writers are also starting to stand out and head overseas. If you're thinking of inviting Japanese writers to your country for a show or a jam you might already be too late.
Only kidding.

KRESS

KRESS / Mito City

INTRODUCTION

Graffiti is everywhere. From its origins in America (New York), it has spread to Europe and the world over, developing and diversifying on the way. With different languages have also come different letter forms and entire new ways of presentation. The internet has played a huge part, with pictures, videos and information accessible to anyone with a computer. Such access has meant style and influence has had the opportunity to spread and grow.

Even with this phenomenal growth graffiti remains the most honest of all art forms. (And that is where our interest lies.) You don't need to pay an entry fee; you can see it up and down roads, tracksides and parks; it is open for anyone to do who is willing to put in the hours; and at the end of the day anyone can criticise it.

The vast and quickly growing cities of Asia have become hives of constantly evolving pockets of graffiti activity, and the continent has become a place that other graffiti writers must visit. Thailand, Indonesia, Japan and Korea all typify how graffiti in Asia is developing and the styles on offer reinforce how honest graffiti is.

This book focuses on Japan – arguably the first Asian country to which graffiti spread from New York. Japan is a country with massive urban and suburban sprawl, making a large portion of the country the perfect graffiti canvas. The capital Tokyo and its suburbs, which run almost into that of neighbouring Yokohama in Kanagawa prefecture, form the largest centres of graffiti activity in the country. However, there are also very active scenes elsewhere, particularly in the cities of Osaka, Nagoya and Hiroshima.

The title of this book is derived from combining the Japanese word *rakugaki* – meaning to scrawl – and the idea of racking paint. This book and DVD documentary shows some of the most influential graffiti in Japan at the moment and demonstrates how far graffiti has developed and spread.

Travelling around Japan meeting graffiti writers, we wanted to capture the vibe of being in these places, but also having the time to actually look at the pieces. By the imagery in the book and the real feeling of each place given in film on the DVD, we really hope that we have created a unique perspective on Japanese graffiti.

A big thanks also goes to all those involved from day 1. ZYS, TABU, KAN and MSC who showed us the real old school Tokyo. CASPER, VERY, ZONE and all the Osaka crew who have showed love and helped show us some of the best spots in Japan.
Also SUIKO, EMAR and TENGA, who recently smashed the UK at AROE's Sleeping Giants Jam, all the RareKind family who continue to inspire every day.
And finally KRESS, without whose help a lot would have never been achieved.

July 2006,
Studio RareKwai, London

VOLT / Hiroshima

/1 /2 /3 /4

ZEN ONE demonstrates how to build a joint cap.

ZEN ONE is a writer from Osaka and is also the main distributor of Scotch caps for writers all over Japan and now Asia.

Back when I started writing there weren't as many imported cans available like there are today, so we hardly ever used foreign cans. But the problem for us was that Japanese cans come with caps with an oval-shaped nozzle so you can spray a wider surface area and you can also switch between vertical spray and horizontal spray. Writers like CASPER use that function well for tags, but it's very difficult to paint a whole piece using a cap like that. What we really wanted was a cap with a circular spray so we could draw nice lines like the New York FAT cap.

We were aware that writers in the US were using New York FAT caps for graffiti and that you could buy replacement caps but we couldn't use them or sell them in Japan because Japanese cans are built differently to foreign cans. With foreign cans you generally insert the cap into the can, but in Asia it is the opposite – there is a bit which sticks out of the top of the can that you insert into the cap.

So I started trying out all kinds of caps from hairspray caps to insecticide caps but still I couldn't find a cap that could produce a perfect outline. I was convinced I could find a Japanese cap suitable for a Japanese can and I used to collect lots of caps from rubbish tips. But when I met COSAONE for the first time he was using what we call the 'joint-cap' technique to fit New York FAT caps onto Japanese cans.

What is this 'joint-cap' technique?

You basically pull out the nozzle part of the Japanese cap with a pair of pliers and insert the New York FAT cap into the hole sideways. When the two caps are connected the New York FAT cap sticks out from the side of the Japanese cap, and when you hold the can down the spray actually comes out from the New York FAT cap on the side. With this technique we were able to get a clean circular spray. This technique was still being used by some writers even until fairly recently.

How did the Scotch cap become the 'cap of choice' for Japanese writers?

One day back when I was still searching for good-quality caps to fit Japanese cans I happened to come across a can of Scotch Guard at home. I tried the cap and it worked really well and I've used it ever since. I began stealing the caps from DIY stores, but as soon as I told other writers about my find they all started stealing the caps too and it became a big problem for the 3M Japan office (manufacturers of Scotch Guard). By then I'd been contacting 3M for a while about distributing their caps to no avail, but one day 3M

contacted me saying there'd been many complaints from DIY stores across the Kansai region about caps from their product being stolen. I told them that if they let me distribute their caps this wouldn't happen anymore and they let me contact their cap manufacturer and start distributing the Scotch caps.

I hear you also distribute Scotch caps across Asia?
Right now I distribute to writers in Korea, Indonesia, Singapore, Thailand and I'm also getting enquiries from China.

How did writers in these countries find out about your Scotch caps?
That's all thanks to VERY sensei. To me he's a graffiti diplomat. I always get enquiries from countries he's

visited. He probably uses the caps and leaves some there. If the writers out there use it and like it they become really desperate to get hold of these caps. To us it may only be worth a mere 50 yen, but in, like say, Thailand where prices are relatively cheap, it must cost them, like, 100 or even 200 yen. Even so, they are always contacting me, so it's a must-have item out there.

What graffiti tools are unique to Japan?
The cheap option for Japanese writers is *bokujyu* [calligraphy ink]. That stuff is really tough! It lasts a long time and if you get it on your hands it's almost as bad as oil-based ink. Calligraphy ink can be rubbed off, but a single drop can spread 20 times its size if it comes in contact with water. It's properly messy

so you've got to be careful, but it's perfect for bombing. Because of the calligraphy culture in Japan calligraphy ink is readily available in super markets, convenience stores and even in 100 yen shops where you get a 180ml bottle.

What is the most popular Japanese spray can today?
The Creative Colour range made by Asahi Pen is probably the most popular spray paint amongst most Japanese writers today. Creative Colour has the most extensive range of colours in Japan, but it's not particularly cheap and it doesn't dry very quickly so it's not very suited to live painting or painting characters, patterns or backgrounds where you have to paint layers.

KRESS
//KANAGAWA

KRESS is one of the most influential writers in the Japanese graffiti scene today and is a key member of the SCA crew from Kanagawa. His styles are many and varied from tags, throw-ups to full-scale production pieces with SCA.
He has painted with writers such as REVOK from MSK as well as OS GEMEOS (The

Opposite / Nikotama

Above / Nikotama
Both pieces are located under the
supports of a motorway bridge on the
border between Kanagawa and Tokyo's

KRESS + AKIM / Unknown location, Okinawa
Piece by KRESS. Character by AKIM from Okinawa.

KRESS / Unknown location

KRESS / Unknown location

Clockwise from top left
Sakuragi-cho, Yokohama, Kanagawa
Nagoya city centre
Throw Up / Sakuragi-cho
Throw-up / Hospital, Kanagawa

BUTOBASK
//KANAGAWA

Another member of the SCA crew, BUTOBASK is one of the few hard-core train bombers in Japan. He is also affiliated with the Tetsujinkai (TGK) who are known mainly for painting trains.

Opposite
Yokohama, Kanagawa

This page from top
Mito City Station
Unknown location
Sakuragi-cho

SCA CREW
//KANAGAWA

Based in Kanagawa, SCA crew is made up of writers KRESS, PHIL, FATE, BUTOBASK and MAKE, and is one of the most prolific production piece crews in Japan. From huge productions to commissions to painting trains, SCA is known to combine their individual styles very well.

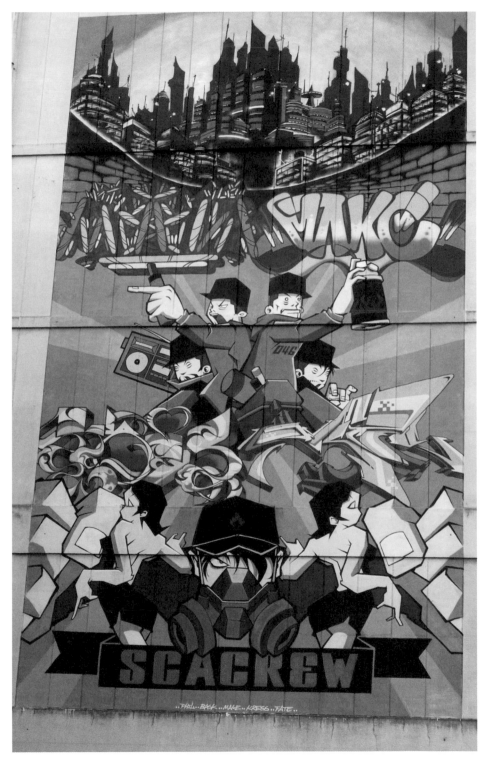

SCA / Production Piece, Mito City
This huge production piece is on a back wall of a
disused department store building in Mito's city centre.

KANE
//KANAGAWA

KANE is one of the first generation of writers to emerge from Kanagawa. Hailing from the Sobudai area of Kanagawa, his style represents a particular form of wildstyle and he paints extensively across Japan.

Opposite
Construction hoardings, Mito City Station

KANE + KAMI / Shibuya, Tokyo
This commissioned wall by KANE and KAMI is
painted on a side wall of an apartment block.

Abandoned Hospital / Kanagawa
Side entrance of an abandoned hospital in
rural Kanagawa.

Above / Nagoya city centre
Right / Nagoya city centre

ESOW
//TOKYO

Affiliated with the WOM (Word Of Mouth) crew and based in Tokyo, ESOW is best known for his unique characters. He has painted with a range of top writers such as KAMI, CASPER, DEPAS and KRESS.

Opposite
Playground, Tokyo
Right
ESOW + KAMI / Playground, Tokyo

Top
Abandoned Hospital, rural Kanagawa
Bottom
ESOW bench / Playground, Tokyo

Clockwise from top left
Sakuragi-cho, Yokohama, Kanagawa
Playground, Tokyo
Character / Tokyo street

SASU
//TOKYO

SASU mainly draws characters and colourful geometric patterns, but she also has a variety of stickers and puts up throw ups around the Nakemeguro area of Tokyo. She is affiliated with Hitotzuki, Barnstormers of the US and has also painted alongside Brazilian writer NINA in London.

Opposite
Production wall / Shibuya, Tokyo

Clockwise from top left
Throw Up / Tokyo street
Sticker / Playground, Tokyo
Shop front / Mito City
Abandoned Hospital / rural Kanagawa

KAMI
//TOKYO

Originally from Kyoto and currently based in Tokyo, KAMI is a member of Hitotzuki and part of the Barnstormers collective of the US. His work can mos[t] be found in and around the Nakemeguro area of Tokyo.

KAMI + KANE / Shibuya, Tokyo
This commissioned wall by KAMI and KANE is on the side
of an apartment block situated in central Shibuya.

KAMI / Sakuragi-cho, Yokohama, Kanagawa

Playground, Tokyo

ESPY
//NAGOYA

ESPY is part of the EDC (Evil Dots Crew), Nagoya and is one of the key members of the relatively uncharted Nagoya graffiti scene. Currently he runs his own graffiti / apparel boutique in the centre of the city.

Opposite
Car park wall / Central Nagoya

Clockwise from top left
ESPY's shop interior / Nagoya
Canvas / ESPY's shop
Interior / ESPY's shop

SQEZ
//NAGOYA

SQEZ is a member of the EDC (Evil Dots Crew) of Nagoya, alongside other writers such as AREL, ESPY, ZECS and VERY. He is best known for his tentacles which can be found on shutters, stairs and rooftops all over Nagoya.

Opposite
Nagoya street

Clockwise from top left
Throw Ups / Oosu, Nagoya
Sakae, Nagoya
Central Nagoya

43

CASPER
//OSAKA

CASPER is a member of the CMK, the most prolific crew to emerge from Osaka. According to ZEN ONE, CASPER's distinctive italic letter styles have evolved from his love of old English fonts. CASPER is also known for his `monster' throw-ups, which can be regularly spotted in the central Ame-mura district of Osaka.

Clockwise from top left
Osaka street
Letters / Tokyo

DEPAS
//OSAKA

Another member of CMK, DEPAS is known for his drawings of dragons and other traditional Asian characters. He also has a variety of throw ups, tags and stickers all over Osaka and Nagoya.

VERY
//OSAKA

Born and bred in Osaka and affiliated mainly with CMK, HS and Nagoya crew EDC, VERY is often described as the Japanese graffiti ambassador. Regarded by many as one of the most travelled writers, VERY has left his mark on cities all over Japan and has been travelling to countries throughout Asia, as well as the US, on graffiti tours (see interview in All Asia, pp. 108-109).

Opposite
Tunnel / Osaka suburbs

Top
Sakuragi-cho, Yokohama, Kanagawa
Bottom
NEIM + MOTEL + VERY / Kanagawa

Left
Trackside Throw Up / Sakuragi-cho
Right
Trackside Throw Up / Tokyo

Opposite
Ame-mura, Osaka

Interview with VERY

When did you start writing?
I started writing 'VERY' at the beginning of '97. Before then I was tagging around my neighbourhood using other names but '96/'97 is when I started writing.

What crews do you paint with?
CMK, HS and EDC from Nagoya. Although I don't just stick to writing with crew members.

Why do most Japanese writers use the English alphabet instead of Japanese?
Personally, I simply started writing 'VERY', but the fact is, it's easier to get your name out abroad if you use alphabet. There were times when I would switch to using *katakana* lettering and foreign writers would tell me it was an interesting shape, but no one could read it. I still use Japanese letters occasionally but I keep my tag in alphabet so everyone can read it. It's an interesting issue, but even in our everyday we are flooded with a lot more English alphabet than people from abroad imagine. I guess for us the most stylish letter around is the English alphabet and I find it easy to write.

Do you have any foreign letter styles?
I have a few. I use Korean *hangul* letters and I went through a phase when I had a Thai style. Otherwise Japanese letters like *katakana* and I also tried *hiragana* for a bit, but it really didn't suit my blocky letter style.

I hear you had some trouble with the vandal squad while in New York?
I'm not certain if they were from the vandal squad, but I was in the Japanese area of New York recently. I looked around the area as usual and started to drop my tag in a doorway when two young guys ran at me. They showed me their police badge and I tried to run for it, but they beat me and smashed up my glasses. I had a friend around the area, but it was my mistake for not having a lookout. They took me in their car and kept me in jail for a couple of days, but they let me off with a fine in the end.

How do the police treat writers who are caught graffing in Japan?
In Japan it's all about money. I've heard of foreign writers who got off very easily, but for Japanese writers it's all about money. It really sucks although I've been relatively lucky so far. I've been let off when I lied saying I work at a paint shop and I can clean the damage for free. Other times I only had to pay 50,000 yen for damage repairs, but one of my friends once got fined 2 million yen just for writing on a shutter.

What is the difference between Tokyo and Osaka?
Compared to Tokyo, Osaka is a small town. In terms of street, Tokyo has a lot more police. I've been caught 6 or 7 times in Japan, of which 3 times was by police in the Shibuya district. Osaka isn't policed as much as Tokyo.

How has graffiti changed in Japan over the years?
A big exhibition on Japanese graffiti was recently held in a national art gallery which would've been unthinkable a few years ago and more people are now publishing magazines and exploring new media. I guess it's a good thing.

Opposite:
Hangul Letter Shutter / Mito City

Top
Stencil / Mito City
Bottom
Worm Stencil / Unknown location

How much if you get caught writing a train?
At least 2 or 3 million yen. The closer it is to a city, the bigger the fine.

Who are the main train writers in Japan?
Writers like BASK, YACK, TABOO, probably.

How hard is it to write on the Shinkansen (high-speed Bullet Train)?
It's not that difficult up in Tohoku area [north Japan] but it's very difficult to get to a Shinkansen in west Japan. Apparently there are yards in

Tohoku where you can just climb over a fence, but in other areas the security surrounding a Shinkansen yard is something else.

What makes Japanese graffiti unique?
I think Japanese characters are unique. I sometimes get characters drawn in my book that I don't particularly like, but when I take it overseas and show my book to writers from famous crews they all seem to be fascinated by the characters most.

ZEN ONE
//OSAKA

ZEN ONE is a member of the NBS (Naniwa Bombing Squad) crew of Osaka.
Together with crew member COSAONE, he pioneered the Osaka graffiti scene
and led the way for crews like CMK to emerge. He is also the main distributor
of Scotch caps to many graffiti writers across Japan and Asia (see interview in
Tools of the Trade, pp. 11-12).

Opposite
Gallery Wall / Mito City

Top
Live Paint / Okayama City
Bottom
Live Paint / OSS, Nagoya

Top
Throw Up / Car pa
Bottom Left + Righ
Throw Ups / Osaka

Opposite
Wall / Unknown Lo
Gallery / Mito City
Gallery / Mito City

Interview with ZEN ONE

Who were the first writers in Japan?
The earliest writers were probably SNIPE from Tokyo or KAZZROCK around '90 or '89. But the first writer to be picked up by the media and fashion magazines has got to be KAZZROCK.
I myself started writing around '92, '93.

What made you start writing?
Back when I started writing, a lot of American culture was coming into Japan. Hip Hop was also starting to get very popular. I was still in high school and I started seeing a lot of graffiti on record sleeves and stuff, which may have been the cause for me to start writing. I was also influenced by films back then like *Wildstyle*, *Beatstreet* and *Breakdance*.

How did you get hold of information on graffiti?
There were places where we could just about get hold of the few graffiti magazines that were around. Back then there used to be a magazine called Can Control and other magazines which only had black and white photos of graff. I looked at rare material; tried to copy it and it did influence me directly.

How does the Japanese media portray graffiti?
I have to say they are trying their utmost to wipe it out. As far as I can see, they have never officially said anything to justify graffiti. But I think it's starting to get more recognition publicly, both as *rakugaki* [graffiti] and as a form of art.

EKYS
//TOKYO

EKYS is a bomber who specialises in hitting up streets and tracksides in Tokyo. His drip tags and stickers can be found all over the city and he also likes large trackside blockbusters, usually to be found along the Yamanote line.

Opposite
Trackside Blockbuster / Meguro, Tokyo

Clockwise from top left
Shibuya, Tokyo
Trackside Blockbuster / Meguro, Tokyo
Tokyo street
Drip Tag / Shibuya
Roppongi, Tokyo

61

QP
//TOKYO

QP is a member of the HS crew and is considered by many to be one of the most prolific bombers to emerge from Tokyo. Tracksides, rooftops, back streets and alleys – his distinctive stickers and throw-ups can be found in nearly every district of Tokyo. Recently he has also been on a tour of Europe, painting with The London Police in Amsterdam as well as Germany and Belgium.

Opposite:
Trackside / Daikanyama, Tokyo

Top:
Trackside / Daikanyama, Tokyo
Bottom Left:
Throw Up / Shibuya, Tokyo
Bottom Right
Throw Up / Bridge support, Tamagawa, Tokyo

Yamanote Line Trackside / Meguro, Tokyo

Clockwise from top left
Mito City
Roppongi Station, Tokyo
Unknown location
Harajyuku, Tokyo

TABU
//TOKYO

TABU is a well travelled writer. He has painted in Australia with BRABE and DMOTE and in the US with the legendary TATS crew. He is also a keen bomber and paints trains in and around Tokyo.

Throw Up / Shibuya, Tokyo

SKLAWL
//HIROSHIMA

SKLAWL from Hiroshima is known for his *hiragana* letter pieces. He also has a good range of characters, and has painted in Korea with ZEN ONE.

Opposite
Car park, Mito City

Top
VOLT+COOK+SKLAWL / Unknown location
Bottom row
Motorway underpass, Hiroshima suburbs

SUIKO
//HIROSHIMA

SUIKO is one of the most influential writers to emerge from west Japan. He is based in Hiroshima and enjoys painting large productions and commissions. Recognition of his skill has brought him out of west Japan to write with renowned writers such as KRESS and BELx2. Unusually his pieces are mainly written in *kanji* (Chinese-style Japanese letters).

Car park wall, Mito City

When did you start writing?
About '99 or 2000, so only for about 6 years.

What crews have you painted with?
I used to write with NSF, but I've left the crew now. The members were all from west Japan and included SKLAWL, CS, T2 and VTR. NSF was a collection of the most active writers in the area.

Unlike most Japanese writers you've chosen to use Japanese letters . . .
Actually, there are a lot of writers who use Japanese letters: SKLAWL uses *hiragana*, and I think CS used to use *katakana*. For myself 'SUIKO' is in *kanji*, while 'VOLT' is in *katakana*.

What is it like to write graffiti using Japanese letters?
I find it very interesting. When I use the alphabet I can't help but think about foreign styles. But since I started writing more Japanese letters, I began to appreciate their unique forms – the fade brush strokes and the energy of the letter. I don't feel that everyone should use Japanese letters, it's just that I personally find it interesting.

I hear you painted in Europe. Where and who have you painted with?
I was in Germany for 6 months and I also visited Italy and the Czech Republic. I mainly painted with a writer called DYSET of the DFM crew. We travelled around Germany in a car for a week writing pieces everywhere we went. I was only in the Czech Republic for a day or two with a German writer called KOBOLT and we went to write in what looked like an abandoned factory. It turned out that half the factory was still running, and we got totally locked in after all the workers went home. It was a mission to break out, but we made it in the end.

School tennis court/ Hiroshima

What do you think of getting paid to do graffiti?
Recently I've been aiming more towards creating murals. There are some writers who seem to keep bombing regardless of their age, but I just can't see myself doing that. I want to be holding a spray can until I die, and I also don't want to do anything other than graffiti. I don't mind working on graffiti-related designs, but I want to do it all on walls. I guess it's normal to have a job and graffiti as a hobby, but I have to constantly be doing graffiti. So my job has to be graffiti. Whether you can call it graffiti or not is another matter, but I'd like to keep doing more pieces.

Are there many writers like you who are based outside of Tokyo and Osaka?
There are writers everywhere across Japan now, but in rural areas it's hard to get reliable information and some writers just swallow what the media says.

What is it like to be a writer outside of Tokyo and Osaka?
There aren't many writers around, so it can get lonely at times. But recently there have been more writers visiting Hiroshima, so it's getting better. Foreign writers contact me, but they always end up just going to Tokyo. I guess it's too rural for them, but my base is Hiroshima and I'm happy to keep it that way.

© TENGA / SUIKO / EHAR ≫2006.

What are your views on the current Japanese graffiti scene?
Considering the relatively small number of writers in Japan, I feel there are many with unique styles. In Europe there are so many writers with killer styles, but many are also very similar in style. In this sense I think the graffiti scene in Japan is very condensed.

Have you painted any trains and what is it like painting trains in Japan?
SKLAWL and CS were into painting trains and I did a few myself. But painted trains in Japan never get to run, so for me that's not very fun. But both BASK and MAKE are really into trains and according to him: it's not about whether the train runs or not, but it's the memory that's important. It's good that everyone has

www.suiko1.com

Opposite
SUIKO + EMAR + TENGA / Hiroshima

Above
SUIKO + SKLAWL / Hiroshima suburbs
(piece by SUIKO, the dragon by SKLAWL)
This piece was commissioned by a
farmer living in the area.
Right
Characters by SUIKO

TENGA
//TOKYO

Tenga is a writer from west Tokyo who is best known for his characters, but he is also known for his interest in painting trains. He visited the UK in July 2006 and took part in the Sleeping Giants Graffiti Jam.

Opposite
Hachioji

Top
TENGA+TZAR+SUIKO+EMAR / Brighton, UK
Bottom Left
School wall / Machida, Tokyo
Shop wall / Yamanashi

EMAR
//TOKYO

EMAR's distinctive style has led him to paint with SUIKO and TENGA.
He has travelled to the UK a number of times and has painted with writers such
as AROE and ANIE (NT), SHUCKS and TIZER (ID).

Opposite
EMAR + TENGA / Naguri Lake, Saitama

Top
EMAR + SUIKO/ Hiroshima

Bottom Left

Originally fr
considered
emerge from
spin tags, p
windows. ZY
a variety of

ZYS Tags / Tokyo streets

Convenience store, Tokyo

ZYS Tags / Tokyo street

www.suiko1.com

SHIBUYA
Tokyo

The Shibuya district of Tokyo is one of the most hit spots for graffiti in Tokyo.
In the back streets of Shibuya is this production wall which is a collaboration
between local writers such as KAMI, SASU, KRESS and Brazilian writers such as
OS GEMEOS and NINA.

Above
Characters / OS GEMEOS
Left
KAMI

YOYOGI PARK
Tokyo

Yoyogi park is one of Tokyo's few open green spaces. These walls in the park
were part of a commission in 2005 and feature writers KRESS and SUIKO.
Characters on both walls are by BELx2 – an old school writer from Tokyo.

Opposite Page
KRESS + BELx2

This Page
SUIKO + BELx2

SAKURAGI-CHO
Yokohama

The railway underpass of Sakuragi-cho in Yokohama is regarded as one of the first halls of fame in Japan. Under the JR (Japan Rail) train tracks, this long wall is covered in pieces by writers old and new, from home and abroad. There are plans to demolish the tracks in the near future, but so far the wall still remains.

MITO STREETS
Tokyo

Mito City in Ibaragi prefecture lies to the northeast of Tokyo. In the autumn
of 2005, the Mito Contemporary Art Centre sponsored the X-Colour Graffiti
exhibition – one of the first graffiti exhibitions to solely feature Japanese writers.
The pieces pictured here are all productions produced for the exhibition.

Opposite
ESOW + KRESS + DICE + DEPAS
/ Car park

Clockwise from top left
SKLAWL + KRESS + SUIKO + BELx2
/ Car park
PHIL + MAKE / Mito City Station
Unknown / Shutter
FATE / Mito City Station

NIKOTAMA
Tokyo

Located under one of the many bridges that cross the Tama river on the Tokyo / Kanagawa border, this spot has pieces by writers from the Kanto region (ie. eastern Japan) as well as well-known writers from the US and Australia.

TUNNELS
Osaka

A secret disused tunnel on the outskirts of Osaka has a number of pieces by writers mainly from the Kansai area (ie. Osaka, Kyoto, Nara).
A few hundred meters in length, the tunnel is a precious piece spot for writers in Osaka who suffer from the lack of walls to paint in the city centre.

'When the university was being built there were plans to have the tunnel as the front entrance, but the plan was scrapped and the tunnel was left. Apparently there have been some suicides in the tunnel, so not many people go there, but it's a good spot nonetheless.' VERY

ABANDONED HOSPITAL
Kanagawa

Located in rural Kanagawa prefecture is this abandoned hospital which is regularly painted by local writers.
For the general public it is also known as one of the most haunted places in Japan.

'The place is famous throughout Japan for being haunted. I've heard around 5 people have been murdered there. I don't write there because I swear I get ill whenever I paint there.'
BUTOBASK

OSAKA
STREETS

TOKYO
STREETS

Japan Rail

BUTOBASK, of SCA and Tetsujinkai (TGK), is one of the few hardcore train bombers in Japan.

When did you start writing?
1997.

How often do you go writing?
Every month. I'm graffiti every minute, every second. Aren't we all?

Why are there so many good writers based in Kanagawa?
I think it's because Kanagawa is an area that has all the elements of graffiti from tags, city bombs to train bombings. There are many writers in Kanagawa who hate losing. Everyday is STYLE WARS.

Are there many writers who like painting trains?
The train scene in Japan has a long way to go yet and so I feel we have to try and communicate to the other writers the thrill of hitting trains. AMES, TOMU, DWES are all my homies from Tetsujinkai (TGK), which specialises in train bombing – number one in Japan.

Is it hard to break into a train yard in Japan?
I think it's pretty easy. It's more exciting the harder it is to break in.

Do painted trains ever run in Japan?
Sometimes they do, but they get buffed straight away by the authorities.

What do you have to watch out for when you paint trains in Japan?
I think it's about being or not being able to read the atmosphere of a yard. I only go with writers who I really get on with because it can end up being a big problem.

Why do you like painting trains?
I like painting trains because unlike other types of bombing, every action remains in my memory. I get flashbacks of the air, the atmosphere, the smell. Don't other writers feel that too?

Have any writers ever targeted the Shinkansen (high speed Bullet Train)?
As far as I'm aware, KOBOLT from Berlin and DOUS2 from Sendai, Japan have.

KOBOLT's bombing was picked up in a big way by the media. It really influenced me. DOUS2 is also really dope, he's one of my favourite writers.

Do foreign writers go for trains?
It seems like some writers do paint trains while they're in Japan.

Have you ever painted abroad?
I've never been abroad.
I have to conquer Japan first.

Do you use Japanese cans? Or foreign cans?
I use Japanese cans. I can't rack foreign cans because they don't sell them at the DIY store. I like cans made by Asahi Pen.

Ever been caught graffing?
Not once. Not even for racking paint. I've never thought about getting caught.

What do you most like about graffiti?
When I get praised for what I do and meet others that are safe. Also being able to meet likeminded writers.

What does it take to be a 'king'?
Personally I'm not very interested in the title of 'king', so I'm not sure but maybe it's about how much you can perfect your original style. I think everything starts there. If you can find a truly original style that is unlike any other in the world then you are already a king. How's that?

Opposite
TENGA / Tokyo

Clockwise from top left
BUTOBASK / Unknown Location
TENGA / Unknown Location
BRABE+SET / Yamanote Line, Tokyo
SUPAFLIE / Hankyu Line, Kansai

VERY Throw Up / Jakarta, Indonesia

All Asia

Interview with VERY

I hear you paint a lot in Asia?
Yes, I use the internet to contact writers in Asia. So far I've been to China, South Korea, Thailand, Philippines and Indonesia. Other than Asia I've been to the US about 4 times.

Did you see many writers from overseas?
The country that most writers from US and Europe visit seems to be Thailand because it's a cheap place to have fun. There are many places where writers from overseas have left pieces and so Thai writers influenced by that are technically good. In my view the most graffed nation in Asia may be Japan, but Indonesia definitely comes close. Indonesia is amazing; I went there not expecting much and was so

surprised. Indonesia was full of pieces – from toy to skilled. The police are very friendly there and they'd even come and talk to us while we painted, so it's easy for anyone to write.

What is the scene like in South Korea?
There's only legal graffiti. The writers in South Korea don't do illegal pieces and reject illegal graffiti. Maybe it's because they have to go on national service but they all seem close to their country. There isn't much 'anti'. But they really like to drink, so they come tagging with me when they're drunk.

What about China?
There is some graff. I once went to Shanghai believing a big city would have graff, but there was hardly any.

Did you see many foreign writers in Indonesia?
Jakarta was pretty much untouched by foreign writers, but in Bali there are lots of surfers so I saw some pieces by Australian and American writers.

What paint do you use in Asia?
I use local Asian cans because I can fit Japanese caps. Indonesia and the Philippines have pretty much the same can called Pylox made by a Japanese manufacturer. Thailand, China and South Korea each have their own brand of cans.

How do Scotch caps fit to other cans in Asia?
When I visited South Korea for the first time I took some Scotch caps with me and now they have become a necessity over there. I think the majority of writers in Thailand use Scotch caps too now.

VERY Boat / Bali, Indonesia

PHOTOGRAPHY CREDITS:

p.9 Volt / p.11 Zen One / p.13 Suiko / pp.16-18 Kress / p.21
Kaze Magazine / p.22 Kress / p.41 Espy / pp. 44-46 Sanei Art
Studio / pp.51-52 Very / pp.56-57 Zen One / p.59 Zen One /
pp.71-72 Suiko / pp.74-75 Volt / p.76 Suiko / p.78-81 Tenga /
p.82-84 Zys / p.86 Zys / p.102 Sanei Art Studio / p.106 Tenga /
p.107 Kress+Tenga+Supaflie / p.108-109 Very /

All other photography by Suridh Hassan, Ryo Sanada and iloobia.

ACKNOWLEDGEMENTS:

Kress, Suiko, Tenga, Zen One, Very, Sanei Art Studio Osaka, Swyfto
@ Gokai Nakameguro, ZYS, Jo Lightfoot & Donald Dinwiddie @ LKP.

Also our deepest gratitude goes out to;

Casper, Depas, Namachu, DYZ-exp, Oriental Street Service Nagoya,
Koolaid, Ken, DJ Matsu, Shingo Sakaida, Pai @ DYZ-exp,
Kaze Magazine, Drawamok, Tatsuki, DJ Quietstorm,
DJ Wessun and Do-Hyo Orizin,
Goth-Trad, Kazuhiro Tagami, Andrew Edwards, iloobia,
RareKind and all the Fam.

http://

www.kazemag.com
www.suiko1.com
www.driphomeworks.com
www.cmkru.myfws.com
www.hitotzuki.com
www.imaone.com

www.dyz-exp.com
www.oriental-s.jp
www.shizentomotel.com
www.belx2.com
www.scacrew.org

WRITER INDEX:

ABOUT THE AUTHORS:

Studio RareKwai (SRK) is an independent cross media production company specialising in the promotion of international music and culture through documentary production, film and publications.
Our team consists of international individuals originating from Japan, India, South America and Europe, giving us unique access into a variety of areas.

SRK's first self-produced documentary film on Japanese Hip Hop culture 'Scratching The Surface: Japan', featured on the award winning French television show; 'Tracks' (22/04/2004,ARTE) and was subsequently televised across Europe in April 2004. This was immediately followed with successful screenings at the 12th Raindance Film Festival in London, the Leeds International Film Festival and the Vancouver International Hip-Hop Film Festival.

// Ryo Sanada
Born in Manchester and having spent much of his early life in Japan, Ryo now lives in London where he is the Creative Director of Studio RareKwai.

// Suridh Hassan
Suridh was born and bred in North London and having spent much time abroad, now resides in West London. Currently Suridh is at Studio Rarekwai as Head of Development and Director.